Make Money Blogging

*Your Clear Path to $10,000
Per Month and Beyond*

Table of Contents

Introduction

Congratulations on downloading this book and thank you for doing so.

This is an excellent time to start blogging! We live in a society where people want more. They are unhappy with their jobs, they want more things, more to keep them entertained. People are forever in search of the "American Dream". Good news! You can reach that dream by blogging!

Blogging has turned into a lucrative endeavor and so many people are beginning to blog in their free time. Some go on to make a good living doing it; others even quit their nine-to-five jobs just to blog. You see it all the time on social media. So how do you become part of that group? How can you make money from home, all while writing about whatever you choose?

This book will help you with everything you need to become a successful blogger. It starts with how to set up your blog and goes into how to make money blogging. It will discuss the methods used to get your blog noticed and all the ways you can monetize your blog so that you can bring in a nice monthly income. Whether you choose to quit your regular job or not is up to you. But this book will give you the tools you need to turn blogging into your career.

There are a lot of websites and blogging coaches that offer their expertise on how to monetize your blog. Hopefully, this book will answer enough questions so that you won't have to shell out hundreds of dollars on advice or workshops.

There are plenty of books on this subject on the market, thanks again for choosing this one! Every effort was made to ensure it is full of as much useful information as possible, please enjoy!

Chapter 1: What Is a Blog?

It's all everyone talks about these days. Blogs. Everyone and their cousins have one, except maybe Grandma and Grandpa (they just don't get it, do they?). Everywhere you look someone is sharing blog posts or talking about blogs. I'm sure you've seen the posts that make their way around Facebook talking about how to manage your life for ultimate bliss, or how someone walked away from their nine to five jobs to travel the world. And I'm sure you've seen the posts about how someone is making so much money blogging, she quit her job, moved to some tropical island, and lives the good life on some white sandy beach with a computer in her lap, and you too can make thousands in a week! Oh wait, I'm getting ahead of myself here.

Look, I am not here to blow that smoke up your butt. Those bloggers put in a lot of time and effort into getting their blogs and life where they are today. If you want to make just a little extra income or be able to retire at an early age, you will have to work hard on blogging. But this is a wonderful time to start a blog! At the very least, it will teach you to write well, connect you with others, and give you a sense of purpose in your life. At the most, you could make a career of blogging and make good money doing it! But to do all that, we need to start with the basics.

So, what is this blog thing? A blog is essentially a personal website that someone uses to post articles, thoughts, and short stories on whatever they choose. I am sure you have heard of <u>Huffington Post</u> or <u>TMZ</u>. If you've been living under a rock for the past couple years, go ahead and click on those links and see what I am talking about. Those sites are blogs! Blogs can be informative, educational, entertaining, or downright weird. If there is something to be said, someone is blogging about it. Some blogs are huge and have multiple staff members while others are run by just one person. Some bloggers use their blog as a platform for their business, others use it as a way to be heard. Everyone uses them for different things, and they all have the ability to make money with them.

It seems so simple, doesn't it? Blogging can be basic, or it can be elaborate. Absolutely anyone can start a blog now and, why shouldn't they? We all put our personal thoughts and pictures out there on social media anyway. Instead of treating Facebook friends to a lengthy post about the cute things your eight cats did today, why not write an article about cats and all the cute things they do? Then you can always share the link on Facebook if you're worried people will miss out on all those adorable cat photos. Blogging has made it easy to get your ideas out there in the world in a productive way that can potentially earn you money.

Is blogging right for you? Seeing as how you have purchased this book, odds are, blogging is for you. But, of course, there are some questions to ask yourself if you want to really be a successful blogger.

- Do I have the time to devote to working on my blog? You will need to not only create blog posts, but you will need to constantly work on research, marketing, and regular maintenance. Blogging can require as much time and energy as a full-time job if you really want to make money with it.
- Do I have the discipline to blog? Blogging takes a lot of work to get started. Can you devote your energy to it and stay focused on what you need to do? Can you really hone your time management skills and force

yourself to work on it when you may not always feel like it?

- Do you have a passion for something and just want to share it? Having a strong drive for something will show in your blog, and people will respond. If you have that passion, this is for you.

- Do you offer something that people are looking for? What do people want that relates to your passions? Would people be interested in what you have to say?

If you answered yes to any of those, then you should definitely start a blog! People love to read a personal perspective on a wide range of topics. If John Smith wanted to know the basics of hunting, he could take a class or consult a manual. But John Smith wants to know what other hunters are talking about, what tips and tricks they have. So, John Smith looks for a blog because he wants a personal opinion. You could be that opinion he seeks. People like knowing that they can read personal experiences and gain unbiased (or biased depending on what you are looking for) information that they might not be able to get anywhere else.

Does blogging still sound fun? Is it still something you want to do? Are you excited to get your blog up and running? Great! Let's keep going!

Chapter 2: Your Blog Niche

I know you wanted to see how to get your blog up and running now. Slow yourself down though. The most successful bloggers start with a plan before they launch a blog. You can't launch a blog without having some idea of what you want to talk about. And those same successful bloggers don't blog about just anything. Here, we will get you thinking and figuring out what it is you are going to write about.

The best blogs out there have a niche. What is a niche? I'm so glad you asked. A niche is a narrowed down area of interest that you can focus on. A niche can be just about anything, provided all the contents are related to that niche. Here is where you will need to brainstorm because it is not always easy to find your own niche.

Let's go back to your passions. What are the things you are most passionate about? If you really love books, you can review books for your blog. Are you a crazy cat lady? You can blog about your cats or advice for other crazy ladies. The possibilities are endless. Yes, you can even write about adult toys, if you chose to. Take some time and think about the things you just love so much you could write about them daily. Be sure to come up with lots of ideas for this.

Before you decide on which niche you want to stick with, you're going to have to do some research. I know, work. I warned you though. Go online and see what other people are saying about your niche. If you picked gaming as your niche, odds are, there are already a lot of blogs and websites devoted to gaming. The market for gaming blogs may be so saturated that it will not be easy to gain some footing in that world. This doesn't mean you must completely give up on the gaming idea. There may be a smaller following of PC gamers that may be easier to reach.

Your niche should be somewhat unique, or else you will drown amongst the other bloggers. You will need to think about the fact that the internet is saturated with mom, fitness, cooking, and entertainment blogs. Yes, this can be a problem, but don't let that deter you. Try to focus on what aspect of the niche you could focus on instead. Did you really want to blog about movies? Try instead to write about certain types of movies. Just because there are a lot of people blogging about some specific thing doesn't mean you can't. You just need to really get creative.

There are millions of bloggers out there right now. That's a lot of people doing exactly what you are trying to do. They are all competing with each other to gain readers. I am not saying that you don't have a chance to do some great things with your blog. But if you want to do those great things, you are going to have to come up with unique and interesting content. Your niche needs to be focused and narrowed down so much that you are now doing your own thing. Instead of focusing on books in general, choose a genre and stick with it. Go even further and blog about only paperback books. Narrowing it down even more, blog about one author you are fascinated with that readers will want to stay updated on.

Want to blog about mom stuff? There's a lot of moms blogging about mom stuff. You will need to narrow it down so that you stand out. What about being a mom can you talk about? You can add some snark to it and talk about the things about motherhood that bug you. All the other mom bloggers blog about happy moments. Go ahead and create a blog about the gross things no one likes to talk about. Moms everywhere would follow because they know they can be a part of something they can relate to.

A market that hasn't been saturated yet is the horror market. Sites like <u>Horror Freak News</u> and <u>I Dream of Screaming</u> are reaching people because there simply aren't a lot of sites like them. There are a lot of travel sites out there, but only a few offer travel coaching. Annie over at <u>Soulful Travels</u> has created a unique blog that not only talks about her travels but offers coaching for those who need it. That's more unique and people love that kind of stuff!

Crafting is really gaining momentum as well. People love creating their own masterpieces and if you are crafty, why not get aboard that train while it's still taking off? If you knit, create a blog full of knitting patterns. Maybe you create unique pieces of jewelry, or you want to teach people how to make wooden benches. There are a lot of options and all of them can make your blog take off.

Something you will also need to start thinking about is the problem you can solve for your readers. Why should they come to your site? What questions could they be asking that you can answer? Do your future readers want to know how to give all eight of their cats fun, themed names? That is a problem that you could answer on your cat-lady blog. Potential readers may need to keep updated on what indie films are playing in their area. That means you can still write about movies, but maybe narrow it down to independent films in major cities.

Now, what to name your blog... After you have figured out what your blog will focus on, you will need a name. You'll want to pick something that stands out and informs people what your blog is about. And of course, you'll want to make sure the name isn't already taken! There are lots of sites that offer to check the availability of domains for free. Here are some sites you can use to make sure what you want to use is available: <u>Google Domains</u>, <u>WordPress</u>, and <u>DomainsBot</u>.

You may want to stick with .com names as well. While there are a lot of domain extensions such as .net, .co, and .org, .com is far more recognized and easy for people to type out. Society has gotten used to most websites being .com's and you may as well stick with it. Being unique is great, but having a .co will just confuse people and they will try to add that extra "m" on the end anyway.

You can also check out <u>this article</u> on how to choose a domain name. Basically, you want to make sure that it is easily pronounced, that you can brand it and that it is a .com. You will also want to make sure it is not too similar to other site names out there or else you could be facing legal action. If you have doubts about it, either find a new name or modify it enough that it doesn't sound too much like someone else's. Don't go creating a site called Bisney and make it about your favorite Disney movies. Use common sense, please.

Take your time with your niche and domain. Remember, the name "Butts R Us" will stick with you as long as your blog is up and running, and let's be honest, no one would ever let you live it down. Choose something that speaks to you and that you will proud of in the long run. You want to treat this blog as if this is the one, the blog that will launch your blogging career and feed your retirement fund.

Getting to Know Your Ideal Reader: This step may seem odd at first, but it is extremely important in getting your blog ready. You must get to know your ideal reader. You want to know who you are writing to. This will help you come up with content specifically for those readers. It will feel like you are leaving a lot of people out, but that is okay. The idea is to build a connection with the specific type of people you want to subscribe to your blog.

Start thinking of your ideal reader as one single person. Who is this person? Give him or her a name. What does he like to do for fun? Does she have kids? How old is your reader? What gender are they? What does your reader look like? What level of education does he have? What kind of job does she hold? Think about what your reader wears, where they shop, what kind of income they have, and how they spend their money.

Get to know your ideal reader very well. Think about every aspect of their life. Is he or she someone you would be friends with? When you really start to think about these things, you will get a better sense of who you will be writing to in your blog posts. You will then write each post as if you are writing to that one person. Before you know it, you have a following of ideal readers who are all like the one you came up with.

To really gain some insight into who your target audience is, you really want to become a part of that audience. Think about who you would have to become to be a part of that group of people. This will help you to think about the target audience and reader in a new way. It will also help you to come up with good, quality content later on.

Remember to stay flexible. You may come up with an ideal reader and write posts for that reader, but get no traffic at all. If this happens, be prepared to come up with a new ideal reader. People change, interests change, and you need to make sure you can change with them. There are a lot of bloggers who have closed down and started up new blogs to change with the times.

Chapter 3: Getting Your Blog Running

Okay, so you've listed ideas for your niche, and you came up with a killer domain name that no one else has. Now you need to create your website. There are a few options to get your blog up and running, and we will go over them so you have a good idea of what you want.

You will need to use a hosting site to start your blog. Hosting sites help to get your blog created, walk you through creating it, and help customize your blog to your tastes. They "host" your site, basically giving your blog a home base to edit posts and change the layout of your website. The host sites make it super easy to design your website and make it possible to go in and change the code within your site if you know how to do that.

Free Hosting: There are free hosting sites out there that will let you set up a website with them. Sites such as Wix and Weebly will allow you to start your blog for free and help you to create a nice site. The problem with these free sites is they attach their names to the domain. If you wanted the domain name livingdeadhead.com, a site like Wix will turn it into livingdeadhead.wix.com. By the way, that domain is open and unclaimed as of this publication! If you want a more professional looking site and if you want to actually make money with your blog, you are going to want to pay for a hosting site.

There are a few cheap hosting sites such as HostGator and iPage. HostGator has plans ranging from $4.95 a month to $12.95 a month. And while those prices may be tempting, be aware that they still do not offer everything the big boy sites offer. You will still get your domain and the advanced option does offer some of the things you need to get going, there are still better options out there.

Tumblr is another free blogging site. It's a little bit of social media too, which makes it a fun, easy platform. Blogger is free as well, but with these platforms, you do not own your blog. Your domain will look like this: *yourname.blogger.com*. That just doesn't look good, does it? You'll look like you don't want to invest the time or money into your blog to make it successful. I have seen a lot of blogs or even author websites that are powered by Wix or Weebly or even Blogger, and with the site name attached to the domain, it looks like they don't care enough about their site to get a real domain. It also looks like they aren't very successful. Set yourself up for success, make yourself look good, and get paid hosting.

Paid Hosting: With paid hosting, you own your blog and site. You also eliminate any other names in the domain. It is strictly what you want it to be. No doctorsmith.weebly.com for you. Having your own site name without the hosting site attached gives you far more credibility.

SiteGround and Bluehost are two of the best hosting services. Ask anyone with a successful blog who hosts their site, and they are going to tell you it's one of those two. The reason so many people are drawn to them is that they offer absolutely everything you need to start a blog from scratch. You get a domain name, great customer service, and they offer an SSL certification (this means that data on your site will be encrypted so that all confidential information is kept safe and locked away).

Both SiteGround and Bluehost have a few types of subscription plans tailored to what you want to do with your blog. As a beginner, you probably want to choose "GrowBig" for SiteGround, and "Prime" for Bluehost. These plans will allow you to customize your blog and do what you want with it. The amount you end up paying will be well worth it. After all, you will make what you paid and then some! And if you choose a different hosting site, that is fine too. There are plenty of good hosting sites out there, these two are just very popular.

Each hosting site works very well and they both walk you through starting up your blog. Many bloggers will tell you that one is better than the other, and maybe for them, it is. But to be honest, they are so similar it really doesn't matter which one you choose.

Once you sign up, take a moment to look at your control panel. It looks super confusing, but it gets easier as you go. Here, you can see your plan, create domain names, add an email address, and see how much data you are using on your blog. Most hosting sites offer a certain amount of space you can use with them, but it's typically a large amount. Browse around the control panel and use the chat feature or call customer support with questions. For both sites, the staff will be able to help you with any questions you may have. I'm fairly certain the people at SiteGround know me well now; I use the chat feature quite often.

You are going to see a lot of information and software to use, but WordPress is your number one tool. WordPress is one of the best software systems to use for creating blog posts and designing your blog. It is incredibly easy to navigate and offers a theme for virtually every niche. You will use WordPress to create content and awesome articles to attract your readers.

Either click on your domain name or the button that takes you to the administrator panel (your dashboard). On your dashboard, you will see there are sections for everything. Go to "appearances" to sift through themes. You can customize your theme and even get free previews of what your blog will look like before you download it and apply it. There are free themes that can be great to use for your blog. And there are premium themes that allow you to do a little more with your site (they have extra features and customization options).

You are going to want to choose a theme that looks professional and fun. You want something that is easy to navigate and won't confuse your readers. You want them to stay on your site, after all. Make sure the layout looks nice and is easy to use and understand. If you decide down the road that you really don't like the way your blogs look, you can always change the theme anytime. You won't lose any of your content either. The change is safe! So, don't feel like you are stuck with whatever theme you decide to use.

People are "love at first sight" creatures. You are going to want to make sure you page is loved at first sight. Readers are first going to browse the home page and see what the site looks like. They want to see an eye-catching page that draws them in and makes them want to stay. So, choose a theme that can help you set up an ideal landing page.

Play around with the dashboard for a little bit. Get to know it. This is the place where you will control everything that happens with your blog. Write up your first post if you want. Make a test one and see how it feels and looks to write a blog.

You can always delete the post later. Customize your theme and the appearance of your site. You can configure how you want your home page to look, you can add a header or a footer, you can add images and give your site a tagline and add a logo. If you really screw it all up, the nice people working for your hosting site will gladly help you get your site back to normal.

Important Pages: There are a few things you should do right away with your blog after you're done playing around with it of course. You will need a disclosure policy and a privacy policy. Yes, I know this sounds all technical and scary, but it will only help your blog in the long run. Set up pages just for the disclosure and privacy policies so that readers can easily find them and read them.

A disclosure page lets your readers know what you do with the blog. It tells them if you make money from sponsors, accept freebies, or have affiliates you make money from. Readers want to know if you are trying to sell them on something because you are truly interested, or because you are getting paid for it. This is important because it establishes a level of trust with your readers. You are being upfront about what you are trying to achieve with your blog. Not sure what your disclosure should say? There are websites out there that have disclosure generators you can use. Disclosurepolicy.org has a wealth of information about disclosure policies and has a great generator you can use for your site. Simply answer some questions and it generates a policy based on the answers you gave.

The privacy policy page is equally as important. Your privacy policy lets your readers know that any information they give you is protected. Remember that SSL certificate? This is where that comes into play. You need that certificate because it ensures that your privacy policy is telling the truth! It tells your readers that any information they give you is only for your site, such as an email for subscriptions only and payment information for only what they are buying on your site. You can't take that information and give it to anyone else. You can also get your policy made for you with freeprivacypolicy.com. It asks you a series of questions and creates a policy based on your answers.

Yes, the policies are boring and it doesn't feel like you need them yet. But when you start selling things and making money with your blog, you are definitely going to need those policies. It is better to get them out the way now!

Be sure to also create an "About" page as well. This page should be about you and your site. Tell your readers a little about you and what you are hoping to accomplish with your blog. Tell them your name and what your big dreams are. Your readers will want to know what your site is about and what values you have. People want someone they can relate to. Keep your information to the point and stick to wording your readers would use.

Make sure you also set up a way for readers to contact you. This can be a page on its own or you can put it in the footer, or even on the sidebar. WordPress will let you customize where you put your contact information. Setting up a contact form will allow readers to input their information and a section to write their comments. You need to be accessible to readers! They want to know that they can ask you questions and send you information about something you were already writing about. Or maybe they have a complaint. Even if they want to tell you how lousy your site it, you must let them do that. Believe it or not, having this option makes you and your site appear that much better to people.

Customization: When setting up your site, you want it to be visually appealing. Let's face it, the attention span of the average person these days is really short. If your site looks boring right off the bat, you will lose potential readers right away. You must create a unique and fun home page that captures the feel of the entire blog. It's not as daunting as it sounds. You should have already had an idea of what you were going for with your blog. Which means you probably had a picture of what it may look like. Take a look through the themes and find one that gets as close to the feel you were looking for as possible. Within that theme, you can choose new fonts and ways to organize the look of your site.

Don't pick a font that is crazy hard to read. You don't want an entire site to read λικε τηισ (like this). You'll lose readers fast. Pick a font that is easy to follow and won't strain the eyes. Set up your blog to feature images so that it's not all just reading. Your home page should have nice images associated with your blog posts. Try to create a setup that has little blurbs about your posts instead of the entire article. Let the reader choose what articles to read; don't force it on him or her.

All of this can be found in the customization section on the dashboard. Click on it and play around. It will guide you so that you know what each customization means. Many themes will let you customize in real time so that you can see what your images and posts will look like with the theme. You can play around with it before setting it as your theme and settling on the look. Remember, people want something that catches the eye, but isn't too much work. Assume your readers are lazy and have Attention Deficit Disorder! If you set up your blog so that it won't bore people, you will start to gain readers.

Make Sure Your Site is Mobile Friendly: Most bloggers set their blog up on the computer. And it is easy to forget that most people will view your blog from their cellphone or tablet. You could have an awesome blog with nice pictures and a great layout. It's so nice and you can't wait to share it with the world. But then someone goes to look at it on their phone and it's a jumbled mess of items. This happens a lot and many people don't check for it right away.

While you are getting your blog set up, and you are setting up the theme, be sure to look at the different views. There is an option to see what your blog will look like on the computer, tablet, and laptop. Go through this and make sure that the smaller devices will still capture the feel of your blog and that the content is still easy to view.

Google is changing the way it looks for websites to rank. It actually checks for mobile optimization as well as content and views. If your site isn't mobile-friendly, Google will have a hard time ranking it for you.

Chapter 4: Writing Blog Posts

Okay, so you've got your blog all set up and are happy with it. If you're not completely satisfied with your site, that's okay. Down the road, you're going to change it again anyway. Most bloggers go through those phases.

It's now time to start brainstorming. Writing should be fun and informative. Offer your readers something exciting to read that gives them the information they were looking for. Make sure the content you are about to share is worth your readers' time. Start coming up with exciting things to write about and make a list of them. You can refer to the list each time you are ready to start a new blog post. Having a stock of content is important because you never know when you may have a blah moment and feel like you have nothing to write about! It also ensures that you always have content for your blog.

This where that ideal reader exercise will come into play. Your content not only needs to be exciting, but it needs to be written for your ideal reader. If your ideal readers are golfers over fifty, you're going to want to come up with some really great golf posts. If you are blogging about how to become a successful blogger, and your readers are new bloggers, you're going to want to make some posts about how to blog and steps readers can take to become successful.

Still unsure of what to write about? Test your audience prior to coming up with content. Go on Facebook or Twitter, post a little snippet of information about a subject you want to write about, and see if people respond. If you get a lot of comments and likes, go ahead and write a post about that subject. But if no one responds, then you know the subject matter may be a little boring.

When you are ready to start writing, you are going to want to do it a certain way in order to attract readers. The site socialtriggers.com has a great chart that shows you how to write a great article, and you can check that out here. It shows you how to set up your article for success and gives you tips on how to write an amazing, eye-catching post.

Start with the title. Or write it at the end, whatever you want to do (it is your blog anyway). Your title should be catchy and to the point. It has to promise your readers that they are about to read something awesome and new. Is your article one of those trendy list posts? Have a title like "10 Best Names for Cats" or "6 Reasons Your Diet is Failing". If your post isn't list based, then it should answer a question or solve a problem. The title can be a little misleading, and sometimes that controversial title can really grab reader's attention. Have you seen those posts that travel across Facebook that say something like "I Don't Like My Kids," but the article is actually about how much she loves her kids? Titles that really stand out. Ask yourself, "what problem does my reader have that I am about to solve?". Answering that should help give you an idea of what the title will be.

The introduction to your article should short, sweet, and to the point. People get bored fast, and they don't care about some lengthy set up for your post. To be honest, I don't even read the introduction half the time. People want to get to the meat of the post! When setting up your introduction, have the paragraph situated with an image right next to it. This will give readers a good visual and the paragraph will appear short. This will hook readers in and they will want to read the entire article.

Creating list posts for your blog can prove to be highly beneficial for you for now. List sites make a killing in blogging because they offer the reader quick, numbered articles. It is easy to follow a list because it literally directs you where to go and gives you short bursts of information. Check out sites like Cracked.com and you will see that most of their articles are in list form. You'll also see that they always have lots of comments and likes. People love lists!

Your posts need to solve a problem your reader faces. Does your reader need to know which "cat playing the piano" videos are the best? Write up a post called "The Five Best Cat Playing Piano Videos You Need to See". Does your reader need to know tips on making money blogging? Come up with a post titled "Six Tips Pros Use to Make Money Blogging".

You don't have to use lists of course. You can come up with posts that are informative without listing items. Problogger has a lot of useful tips on what kinds of posts you can come up with, such as "How to get more from..." or "My least favorite...". The title should capture the reader's attention and solve their problem. Create a "how-to" post that has to do with your niche, but give it a name that screams out that this article contains what the reader has always needed!

Once you come up with ideas on what to write about, you will want to organize those thoughts into a certain format. This not only keeps your main points and other information organized, but it gives the reader something to follow. People need structured wording so that they can absorb the information easily and it also creates a nice flow for the reader to follow.

You will want to separate sections of information into short, readable chunks of information. Each section should begin with a bold heading that grabs the reader's attention while introducing that section. It should promise your reader that there will be information here worth reading. Are you writing about those crazy cats? Feature a subheading that says something like "Cats Make the Best Companions". It's authoritative and will appeal to your cat-loving fans. Each subheading after that should have something to do with the information being presented. If you were to take out all of the extra content, the reader should have a pretty good idea of what your article covers with just the headings alone.

After your first subheading, the content should appeal to the reader's emotions and hook him or her into the rest of the article. Play on the reader's heartstrings. "Cats Make the Best Companions" should have an entire section below it, talking about how adorable cats are, how intelligent they are, and so on. Your readers, the other cat people out there, will have emotional reactions because if they're reading it, they probably also have cats. And they will think of their adorable little critters while they read your post. This is perfect for you because while the readers are gushing over the cuteness of kitties, they are actually getting sucked into the rest of the post.

It isn't necessary, but it would also be helpful to have quotes from your writing that stand alone, with an option to share. People like to post quotes on social media. It makes them sound smart, witty, or like they just know what's up about everything. This can be to your advantage if you set up the button. People will quote you, which will only send traffic back to your site!

You can also create a section within your post that's a sort of "how-to" for whatever you are writing about. Tell people how they can adopt a kitten, or where they can go to get the most adorable little cat bed. Giving your readers a thing to do, something they can actively participate in will boost loyalty and incentive for them to continue reading your posts. People in general like being told what to do. I'm not saying you need to be demanding, but if you give them a task or tell them how they could do a task if they want, they are likely to do just that.

Remember too that most people like visuals. They came to your site to not only read things but see images as well. Insert images, video clips, or sounds into your posts as needed in order to add to the visual appeal of the post. Your first section should have an image that corresponds to the content, but one that helps trigger an emotional reaction.

At the end of your post, create a "call to action" for your readers. Ask them if they liked this post, and if so, subscribe to the site. Say something like "Did you enjoy this article? Stay up to date by subscribing below", and set up a subscription option. This lets readers know that if they liked this one, there is plenty more to come. Let them know they can follow you on Twitter and Facebook. Tell them you'd like to hear from them and make it sound personal. Experiment with wording your call to action as well. Instead of saying "subscribe by email", try something like "get more followers here" or "get your membership here". This type of call to action gets more subscribers and gets attention.

Be sure to also backlink to archived posts within new posts. Create a link within new posts that will direct your reader back to an older post. You can stick this at the end of the new post if you would like. Say something like, "If you liked this post, make sure you check out [older post]." Slip the links within your new post as well, if it fits with what you are talking about. Don't set up a link to an old post about Halloween into your new post about Christmas. It probably doesn't flow smoothly.

Remember that you want content that is memorable here. When writing your posts, ask yourself, is this something I would share with friends? Is it something quotable? Can people read your content and pick out noteworthy statements to share on social media? If the answer is no, start thinking about what you can say that would make people want to show your post off to others.

Once you have edited and finished your post, publish it. Congratulations, you just published your first actual post! But now what? What comes after the initial publication?

Chapter 5: Marketing Your Blog

After publishing, your post sits there on your site. When you first launch a website, odds are you won't have a following right away. You're going to need to gather readers if you want that amazing post you just created to get some recognition. Marketing your blog is extremely important or else how will you get subscribers? You also need to have subscribers if you want your blog to make any kind of money. It would be great if you could just rely on dumb luck, but that's just not how it works. Yes, there is more work ahead, but you will have fun with it.

It should be noted that you can set up your site so that when you publish a post, it gets automatically shared on social media sites of your choosing. This feature can be very helpful. But if you use this method, make sure the shared post says what you want it to. Take the time to set it up each time you publish a post. Some people like that method better, especially after becoming more successful. There isn't a whole lot of time in the day to individually share your post on each social media site.

There are, however, several bloggers who will tell you not to automate your social media sharing. Twitter only lets you use one hundred and forty characters per post. This means your share must be short and to the point, with room for the hashtags you want to use. Facebook lets you use all the characters you want. You'll still want to keep your share shorter, but you have more wiggle room for a better description of what you are sharing. Instagram needs a picture to be shared, and Pinterest is its own beast. It may be more time-consuming to share to each site individually, but sometimes it can be well worth it.

Social Media Marketing: Social Media (you know, Facebook, Twitter, Instagram, etc.) can be a major source of subscribers. You're already on Facebook all day long (come on, you know you are), so why not use it to your advantage? Social media is a fantastic way to connect with potential readers. Yes, your first subscribers will probably be family and close friends. No, that's not as pathetic as it sounds. Subscribers are subscribers.

Twitter, Instagram, and Facebook have an advertising feature you can use to promote either your entire site or a singular post. This is not free, however, but there are reasonably priced options. Advertising on social media can be really helpful. Set up an ad and let it run for a bit. You can choose your plan options and duration of the ad on each social media site. You can get a lot of clicks and likes this way.

You shouldn't completely rely on social media, however. Paying for advertisements constantly will drain your bank account really fast, and you don't always get loyal followers this way. If you are just starting your blog, you will want to focus on organic growth. Organic reach is when people find your content without paid advertising. I know, I know, but how will you get your blog out there if you're not making advertisements?

One big thing you are going to want to learn is hashtags. Or as some of you know them, the pound sign (#). Hashtags are what everyone uses to connect different themes and ideas. Have you heard of #MotivationMonday? Search it sometime in any social media outlet, and you will find a ridiculous amount of sickeningly peppy, motivating pictures and quotes. Hashtags are how people find things they are interested in and see what others are saying about them.

Each time you publish a blog post, share it on social media. On Twitter, it's automatically public, but on Facebook, it's not. Make your posts about your blog public on Facebook, then add hashtags that relate to your target audience and the blog post itself. Still writing about cats? Each time you post a link to a cat article, hashtag it with words like #cutecats, #crazycats, #kittens, etc. Anyone who searches for cat posts will eventually come across your cat posts.

At first, it feels weird to promote yourself so much. Most of us are taught from a young age not to brag. But in the blogging business, you pretty much have to brag all the time. Not only that, but you have to do it in a way that doesn't say, "Look at me! I'm the best!" You should get it out there that this is what you do, that your niche is what you are interested in, and that people will want what you have to offer. It's okay to talk yourself up a bit but don't be condescending. You want readers to start thinking about you when they see something that involves your blog and niche. When someone sees a cat, let them be reminded that you have a great cat blog and then maybe they will go and check it out.

Another social media technique to use is to start getting involved with the community. Get on Twitter and start following people who share similar interests. Find people who share your love of books, or other bloggers in your niche. Twitter users almost always follow you back! Find groups on Facebook that may be interested in what you have to offer, and join those groups. Even if only a few people find you at first, that's okay. We all start somewhere. Remember too that every person who finds your blog and likes it will most likely tell someone else that they should check out your blog as well.

Pinterest is kind of a big deal now. It used to be so simple, but now it's grown into a trendy way to market yourself. Get to know Pinterest. Create an account just for your blog. Start boards that have to do with your niche and add your blog posts. Come up with creative board names and pin regularly. Make you're your blog name is listed on your profile so people can easily see it when they check out your profile. Write in fun descriptions when you pin and don't over promote your blog either. Pinterest can get you a lot of followers and subscribers. All you need are some great pictures and good content. Follow others and they will follow you back.

Make sure that your blog name and URL is on your profile of every social media account you have. Set that part of your information to "public" and make it as bold as you can. When people look at your profile to see who you are, make sure they see you have your own website. If they like the content you share on social media already, they are likely to follow the links to your blog as well.

Remember that blogging can feel a lot like a popularity contest, but you still need to keep the social media aspect of it. Not only will marketing on social media get you subscribers, but it builds a hefty group of followers on each platform. This will come into play later when you want to get advertisers to work with you. You are going to want to show sponsors or advertisers that people listen to what you have to say.

Create a Facebook page just for your blog and invite everyone you know to like it. Share the link to your page on other social media platforms and be sure to direct people to your page when the situation calls for it. Having a well-liked page will only benefit you when you are trying to make money blogging. Make sure that the page has great content and does not just have links to your latest blog posts. Be a person, tell jokes, and try to stay within your niche as much as possible. But people enjoy seeing that you are a normal person and it's not all about the blog for you.

You can also start up a Facebook group just for your blog or for your niche. Get people involved with your blog or the niche. If you are blogging about blogging, set up a Facebook group just for your subscribers or for other aspiring bloggers. If you blog about dogs, start up a group all about dogs, peoples' love of dogs, or useful dog owner tips. People like to get involved and feel like they are a part of something. Set up a group for this!

And please, don't be pushy with your social media promoting. Letting people know some new information about your blog or the newest post you created is great. But bombarding people with posts about your blog gets boring for followers. Do you like it when friends continuously push stuff in your face (think Lularoe or Beachbody) all the time? Post about your blog once a day, but then engage in building relationships with followers and post about other things too. Make sure people see that blogging isn't your entire life.

Email Marketing: Email marketing is probably one of the best ways to make and then keep followers. You create emails and send them out so many times a month (not every day!). First, you will need to find a site that you can use to create popups, opt-ins, and emails. ConvertKit and MailChimp are two very popular email marketing tools. MailChimp has a completely free option that works very well if you are not making money yet. ConvertKit is a paid subscription but offers a lot more for your marketing needs.

When using these tools, you will want to set up some kind of opt-in for your blog. You can create a simple "subscribe" button for your site. One of the best opt-ins is the pop-up form. This is a window that appears on your blog for viewers after they have been on a page for a certain length of time. You can choose a pop-up to come up after a visitor clicks on a link, or after they have been on a page for ten seconds. The pop-up is great because it's not something your followers will miss. It shows up right in front of them and they can opt out, but at least the option is right in front of their face. Once you have created the pop-up with your email marketing site, you can plug in the code it gives you into the widget section of your blog.

Okay, so you're ready to set up an email. One of the first emails you should get going is the "welcome" email. This email will get sent out to people who have recently subscribed to your blog. It gives your subscribers some more information about you or the blog. It could contain an incentive you offered (we will get into this soon) or ways to reach you. The welcome email will let your subscribers know what to expect from here on out and how often they will receive emails from you. Make the welcome email inviting and friendly. After all, you are welcoming a new subscriber home to your community. Let them know what they can expect from you and the blog, and that they can find you on social media too.

You should also take the time to set up templates for your emails. Create a basic design you want your emails to look like and save it so that each time you create new emails, the template is already ready and all you have to do is plug in the information. Your email blasts should contain information about the new things happening with your blog such as store news, recent posts, new offers, and ways to share! Sending emails to your followers keeps you connected to them on a more personal level. Did you know that you can even customize your email blasts to include the name of the recipients? People love that! It's as if you personally sent each follower an individual email.

Be sure to keep a close eye on your email analytics. Most email marketing companies offer this option. With it, you can see if people are opening emails, clicking on them, or unsubscribing. If you have a large number of people who aren't engaging, you have lots of work to do.

You can use these numbers to better your email marketing. Separate your subscribers into lists such as "store customers", newsletter subscribers", and "second chances". Create more enticing emails for those who don't seem to be interested. Send emails about your latest store updates (if you have a store) to the people who make purchases in your shop.

Your email lists are important. So many bloggers don't focus enough on their email marketing strategies and their blog suffers because of it. Your emails are how you connect with new and returning readers. This is where you can get more personal with your readers and share new things in your life and with the blog. Ask readers to respond to your emails and take time to read through those emails when they start responding. Show them you care and actually take the time to listen to what they have to say. You are building relationships with your email subscribers. This will prompt people to either stay with you or even invite others to join your community.

Remember to be true to your word. If you tell subscribers you will send emails once a week, you better send them once a week. Any more or less than that will drive subscribers away. They want good content that arrives when promised. If you can't keep you word on that, you won't keep subscribers.

How to Get Email Subscribers: To get new subscribers to your email list, you need to be prepared to offer others something. People need to be coaxed a little bit into giving up their email. Everyone is already asking everyone else to sign up for things. And a simple "sign up for updates" campaign isn't going to get you many subscribers. People want to be compensated for their time. What can you offer them?

Time to start thinking about what you have to offer people. Remember when we talked about being able to solve a problem for people? This is where you can really use that information. If you blog about how to make money blogging, you can offer new subscribers a free eBook on how to email marketing. If you blog about cats, offer a special email series about the best ways to train your cat. Do you blog about Bigfoot? Tell new subscribers they will get a special weekly email with top-secret Bigfoot information.

It doesn't matter what you blog about. You need to come up with ways that you can offer new subscribers some kind of special thing for signing up. If your blog has a shop, set up a discount for first-time purchasers if they subscribe to your blog. I'm not saying you have to buy loyalty, but you kind of have to bribe people to at least get them to give your blog a chance.

Comment on Other Blogs: Bloggers are typically awesome people. They understand that it is hard to get your blog off the ground. So, connect with them! Go search for other blogs in your niche and start reading their posts. Then, comment on them. Subscribe if you'd like. Start connecting with other bloggers.

When you take interest in other bloggers, they notice and begin to take an interest with you. They may eventually direct others to your blog for more on a certain subject, or even ask you to collaborate with them. Their subscribers may take notice of your comments and see that you also have knowledge on the information. People are nosy, and they will try to see who you are and what you're all about. Use that to your advantage.

Collaborating: When two bloggers come together for a post, wonderful things can happen. Be a guest post on someone's blog. Lots of bloggers want to work with others so that each blogger can gain new subscribers. You may know more on a subject than a fellow blogger, so why not work together to get you both new subscribers?

Find Communities to Interact With: This means all types of communities that relate to your blog. No, this is not the same as social media. Look, you're going to have to become somewhat of a social butterfly if you want people to follow you. Learn how to reach out to people and build relationships.

Online, you can find forums and sites devoted to whatever your niche may be. There are chat rooms and communities for everything. Yes, you will come across people who won't exactly be your cup of tea, but that's part of the business. Engage in discussions with others and communicate with them. Find out what these people are looking for in regard to your niche. Not only will you gain new subscribers, but you may also get ideas on what you can offer as an incentive for subscribing!

There are plenty of bloggers who stick to blogging from their house and don't want to get social outside of the internet, and that still works fine for them. But I would encourage you to get out into the real world a little more and see where you can promote your blog. If you're a book blogger, and you're near a library, join their book club! It provides you with a space to talk with others who are similar interests and you can promote your blog in person. If you blog about dogs, go to the dog park and start making friends with people. See what they have to say about training, what types of dogs are good for kids, etc. You can learn a lot by interacting in person with others. Have business cards made that you can hand out anytime someone asks you what you do. Give them out at your book club. It is possible that people will take it and throw it away. But it is also possible that someone will take it and look into your blog.

Try to Post Often: You won't be bugging people because they will be subscribed to your emails (unless you set your blog up differently). If you can come up with a post every day or every couple of days, that's great! Having a lot of good content will only help you. Then, when you send out emails, give subscribers a taste of what you have been writing about. Let them choose which articles they want to read, but make sure they have lots to choose from. You want your blog to be entertaining enough to keep your followers happy.

Get to Know Your Analytics: Knowing your stats for your blog traffic is a huge help and will come into play numerous times throughout your blogging career. Google Analytics is a go-to program for many bloggers. Signing up is free and it is worth every bit of time you invest into learning all you can about it. At its most basic, Google Analytics will give you insights into how many people visit your blog and how they are finding your blog. It would be in your best interest to take advantage of Google's free Analytics training courses, which will be offered to you when you sign up. That way, you will learn all the ways to master analytics so that you can use that information for your marketing strategies.

There are analytics add-ons you can add to your dashboard on your site so that you have access to snippets of information about blog traffic. If you see that your organic reach (the people who find your blog without paid advertisements) is very low, you know that you must find a better way of reaching others. Google will tell you where your traffic is coming from, what they are clicking the most, and much more. If you see that your post about the best gadgets of 2017 got a lot of views, but your post on fish tanks had almost no views, then you know you should probably stick to posts like the first one.

Advertising with Search Engines: If you feel like putting the money into it, you can also advertise your blog on search engines like Google or Bing. You can easily set up advertisements with these search engines and choose where the ad will show up. You can choose for your ad to show up with search results or have a display ad set up on other sites as well.

While paid advertising can get you new subscribers and potentially get your blog some notice, you aren't getting organic reach. Remember, organic reach is getting new subscribers through searches or any other method except paid advertising. More organic reach means that you will get recognized by search engines and get ranked higher in search results.

Marketing your blog is a lot of work, I won't lie. But it is very worth it. You need to get your blog out there and you need people to be interested in what you have to say. You cannot make any money if no one is visiting your blog! Even if you are making money through ads and affiliates, you can't make money with no traffic. Some marketing strategies may work better for you than others, and that is okay. You will find your own methods and combinations of marketing that work for you. Use those techniques and if something isn't working, be flexible. Change what you need to change. Good marketing strategies will greatly increase traffic and money to your site.

Chapter 6: Create Your Media Kit

Once you have marketed yourself enough to gain followers and statistics you are proud of, you will need a way to show potential advertisers and sponsors this information. When you try to sell advertising space or want a sponsor for blog content, you will need a way to show them how many followers you have on social media, or how many people subscribe to your blog. One thing that every blogger looking to make money should create is a media kit.

A media kit is basically a blogger's resume. It is a way to show others why they should work with you. The Blog Maven has a really good article about media kits that you can check out here. Your media kit should have a nice picture of you and a little blurb about you. You should also include your logo if you have one. You want to have some of your regular content in your kit. Let your future advertisers know what content keeps your readers engaged with your site. Let them know what subject you write about and which posts get the most traffic.

In the kit, you should start with a little bit about yourself. Let the advertisers know who you are and why you started your blog. Show them you have a passion for what you do, and that you really are a nice person and someone they will want to work with. You want the advertisers to see you as a person with feelings and goals, someone they can connect with. Don't be afraid to brag a little bit. Did you write an article for another blog that got a lot of attention? Tell them that! If you were featured in an eBook or magazine, go ahead and tell them that. I

Your media kit should also include a lot of statistics. Here is where you will need to do some investigating. Check your analytics and look into traffic flows on your site. You will want to be able to show potential advertisers how many visitors you average a month, where your traffic comes from, how much is organic growth, how many subscribers you have, and how many followers you have on social media. Does your Facebook page have thousands of likes? Do you have tens of thousands of Instagram followers? Showcase that information!

If you are a newer blogger, and still do not have tons of followers, simply describe and show your trends. Your statistics should show that you have had growth over the course of so many months. Those stats will give the advertisers an idea of where your blog is headed and what it will look like in the future. Show them that you expect to have one hundred thousand subscribers within the next three months. Sometimes those trends can look just as good as all those huge statistics. After all, you are showcasing how awesome you are going to be, and how beneficial it will be for those sponsors to hop on board while your business is growing!

You will also want to include rates that you are asking for space on your site. Do your research and see what others are charging for ad space on their sites. Reach out to those other bloggers that you built relationships with while working on your killer marketing strategies (are we seeing how this all comes together now?). Other bloggers are usually pretty nice and will most likely tell you what they charge or at least point you in the right direction.

Be sure to come up with a good policy as well. You want to make sure you set boundaries and rules to ensure this is a good partnership. Telling the advertiser your rates is great, but now what are they getting out it? Your policy should tell them the size and location of the space they are getting, how long they have to pay for it, and the duration of the ad. Make sure your policies are ideal for both parties. No one will advertise with you if your rates are high, but are only offered for a day! When in doubt, reach out. There are websites and people who would be more than willing to help you with this. If I could give you exactly what to say in your policy and what to charge, I would. But your blog is unique to you and your niche. It's okay to research what to charge and for how long.

One last thing will really boost the appeal of your media kit is testimonials. This section will be used when you have already worked with other sponsors or advertisers. When you are ready to add this information, simply reach out to those you have already worked with and ask them to write up a testimonial. Odds are, this isn't the first time someone has asked for a testimonial and they will know what to do. A testimonial is a written statement (or video) basically saying how good it is to work with you, and why it is worthwhile.

This is equivalent to the "references" section of a resume. You want to show potential advertisers and sponsors that you have already worked with others and that it was a good experience. The testimonial is the proof.

End your media kit with a call to action. You have given your potential advertiser or sponsor a lot of information to go over, and now you want to conclude it. Let them know how they can contact you and what the next steps are. Don't forget to add pictures and make it look fun. While your media kit is very similar to a resume, it doesn't have to be as boring as one! Make it fun while keeping it on a professional level. Make it look nice like you are someone who you would want to work with. Advertisers want to know that they will be working with someone who attracts a lot of people, and boring people don't have high traffic.

Chapter 7: Make Money with Advertising

You have been patient, and you have worked hard to get to this point. Now it's time to explore your options for bringing in an income. There are multiple ways to earn an income blogging, and all of them require those amazing marketing strategies you have been perfecting. You are strongly encouraged to use multiple income streams because no single source of income will ever be truly reliable. People's interests change and you should be able to change with them. We will go over each way you can earn your income and if you utilize all or most of them, you will be on your way to earning a very nice income.

Advertisements and Banners: Display ads or banners are advertisements you can set up within your blog posts. It is very similar to seeing advertisements in magazines. Oftentimes the ad will be a small video advertisement or a banner, that is positioned in the sidebar, header, or footer of the content. The ads are usually related to the content on your site and each time someone clicks on them, you get paid.

There are several companies that offer ads for your blog. Be aware, however, that you will not get ads if you do not have quality content or enough traffic. A beginner may have trouble with getting ads if he or she isn't very popular yet. You can't have three posts about cats, with only one subscriber, and expect anyone to want to pay you for ad space. It simply doesn't work like that. If you've been practicing those marketing strategies and are bringing in some traffic, you have a much better chance at getting an ad company to work with you.

One of the most popular ad sites is Google AdSense. AdSense does need an application to use their services. Once you have been accepted, you input your information and let them know how you want the ads to appear and where you want them. Companies will bid to buy space on your site for an ad. You can customize how the ads appear and even choose not to use some ads if they really conflict with your values or site. Google then takes care of the rest. When people click on your ads, you get paid, but you can only request your payments once you have accrued a certain amount. Again, it can only benefit you here to have a good amount of traffic on your site.

There are other sites you can use as well, but be aware that some of them can be picky. If you take a look at <u>Beacon Ads</u>, you can get a feel for what you need to do to be considered for ads. If you search through the marketplace, you will see that the bloggers listed all have tens of thousands or hundreds of thousands of impressions monthly. This should give you an idea of what it takes to even get noticed for ads.

Running ads on your site can be lucrative, especially if you offer something truly unique on your blog. If you have a lot of traffic or if you have a unique blog, companies will be competing, even more, to buy space on your site. And they will pay well if they are sure people will be viewing their ads.

Private Ads: Setting up ads on your site does not have to be done strictly with an advertisement company like Google. You can set up private ads with people as well, eliminating the middleman altogether. No middleman means you are paid directly and you can set up your own rate of pay.

Search other niches and see what others charge for ad space on their blogs. What is the going rate for the ad space within your niche? Look at their blogs and see where they put their ads on their pages. Most likely, they are where they are for a reason. Learn from others.

Come up with a great pitch for potential advertisers that really sells them on why they should advertise with you. Introduce yourself to the advertiser or sponsor and tell them a little about yourself. Include a picture that shows how awesome and friendly you are; give them a face with the name. You will also want to use that media kit you created here. A good media kit (as discussed in the previous chapter) shows the advertiser that you are someone they need to be working with. Be sure to research the advertiser you are trying to work with so that you know about them, and use that information in your pitch. Let them know what you like about their company and how you can use that to advertise for them.

Blogger Amy Lynn Andrews recommends that you don't leave space open on your blog or have a space that says, "your advertisement here". All this does is show potential advertisers that you aren't popular enough to have other advertisers. After all, if your blog has enough traffic to get advertisers, you shouldn't have a bunch of open space left over. Did I write advertisers enough here?

Sponsored Posts: You can get an entire post sponsored by a company should you choose as well. Reach out to companies just as you did with advertisers. Only this time, let them know you are willing to review a product on your site. You can receive compensation for the sponsored post or simply get a product free with this method. Make sure the reader knows it is a sponsored post, and don't use this method all the time. People will begin to lose interest if all your posts are sponsored. It starts to look like you have no opinions of your own or that you are paid for everything you do. While you want to get paid, you don't want to be so obvious!

Underwritten Posts: These posts are yours alone. You come up with the idea and write about whatever you want.

But you can pitch underwritten posts to companies. Chose a company and post that would go hand in hand and let the company know they can sponsor that post. It's all your own content and all you have to do it write "brought to you by..." at the end or beginning of your post. Again, this should be used sparingly for your readers' sake.

Newsletter Advertisements: Not only can advertisers buy space on your site, they can also buy space in your newsletters. Maybe you don't want to fill up your pages with advertising, in which case you can always sell space in your newsletters. But you will need to prove that you have a good number of subscribers and that they are opening your newsletters. Those are statistics that you will find in your emailing service. The concept is the same in that companies pay for a certain amount of space and a good location within your newsletter. They give you what they want the advertisement to be, and you plug it into your newsletter. The emailing service you use should also make it easy to get the advertisement into your newsletter.

Reviews and Giveaways: These days, people are relying more and more on product or service reviews. They want to know what the average person thinks of something and we all value the opinion of others. Before you buy something on Amazon, do you take a look at the reviews to make sure what you are buying will be a good buy? This trend has opened up a new world of reviewing and giveaways.

You can partner up with a company and write up reviews for the products. You will get a percentage of the sale or even a small payment for your services. Remember that you are writing up a review to give your readers the best information you can give. You don't need to sell them on the product. Try to review products you have already tried and know how they work. You can even reach out to companies asking for free products to review on your site.

There are sites out there that are just for reviewing purposes. <u>My Subscription Addiction</u> is a site that reviews subscriptions like a box of the month clubs or clothing subscriptions. Many times, they will get sent a trial box for free to review and post on their site. The site also offers discount codes when you sign up for a subscription through them. They give their honest opinions on subscription and a go-to when searching for your next subscription. There are many companies like subscription services willing to send out sample products for reviews. All you have to do is reach out.

Giveaways can also boost your income while also getting you new subscribers. You can get a company to sponsor the giveaway, and this eliminates you having to actually send out a free product. Ask around different companies online and see if they would be willing to work with you on a sponsored giveaway. They offer a product, you promote it and tell people to subscribe to you and the other company for their chance to win, or just to get the freebie.

You can also giveaway one of your own products or host a contest. This drives traffic to your site because let's face it, people love free stuff! If you don't have any products to give away, offer free content, insider information, a service, etc. When you offer things for free, you get more people interested in what you have to offer. Think about all the other companies out there that offer a free version of their products. MailChimp has a paid version and a free version. When you sign up for the free version, you get enough services to get you by. But the premium, paid subscription is where you reap the most benefits. The freebie works as a great lure and will draw people into your blog, prompting them to eventually spend money or at least boost your pay per clicks.

Advertising can earn you a lot of money from your blog. It is so tempting to sell advertising space on your blog because of the good money it can bring in. But think about the different sites that you have come across that have advertisements on them. Sometimes they look cluttered and unprofessional. I have seen blogs that are covered in advertising. The ads get distracting and can slow down your site. You don't want to get bogged down with too many ads. Try to stick to strong ones that really represent what you are doing with your blog. Remember, advertising isn't the only way to make money, so you can be picky about how you advertise on your blog if you choose to advertise at all.

Chapter 8: Affiliate Marketing

Affiliate marketing is when you recommend something and a reader clicks on a special link you provide that takes them to where they can buy the product. When they buy the product using your link, you get a commission. That special link really is special. You get it when you sign up for an affiliate program, and the link is coded with special numbers and characters that are unique to your account. Buying a product through that link puts money in your wallet.

But first, let's get you familiar with affiliate marketing. The first thing you will want to do is find companies that offer products that relate to your niche. There is almost always some type of affiliate marketing you can do with each niche. If you're stumped, Google it. Take a look at other blogs in your niche and see what their affiliate links are (I know, it all comes back to research, doesn't it?). You will be able to tell what posts have affiliate links because the blogger will disclose it first!

There are so many companies that offer affiliate marketing, you just have to find them. First, start with sites you like to use. You can scroll to the bottom of the page and look for a link that says something along the lines of "affiliates" or "work with us". You'll find this link by the "contact" and "FAQ". If you don't see that link, don't be discouraged. Simply contact the company and ask if they offer some kind of affiliate marketing.

Do you blog about how to blog? Your hosting site probably has an affiliate program you can take advantage of. When I was learning how to blog, I followed a link on another blogger's site that took me to SiteGround. When I signed up for SiteGround, that blogger got a commission. Do you write about fashion? There are tons of sites out there that offer affiliate programs for clothing. And then there are even bigger companies like Amazon that have affiliate programs set up so that you can get those special links for every product they have.

Try to look around for sites that offer affiliate programs. Do a generic search, see what you come up with. Then try a more narrowed down search within your niche to see what companies offer those programs. If you would rather use a middleman, you can set up an account with sites like ShareASale or Commission Junction. These networks will help pair you with an advertiser in their marketplace. You can work with these companies to set up terms and accept their offers.

Only choose products that are related to your niche! This is extremely important because it can make or break your site. If you choose products to promote on your blog that are directly related to your site, you will make an income. But, if you choose products that are completely unrelated, you will lose credibility fast. People won't trust you and will start think you are a spammer. If you blog about those silly cats, don't post affiliate links to sex toys. That's a really quick way to lose your readers.

Do not forget to let your readers know that you have affiliate links in your posts. You can write up a quick disclaimer right at the beginning of your post, giving your readers a heads up. You should also have this information within your disclaimer policy as well. It is important to let readers know when a post has links that could potentially make you money. This is a little different than a sponsored post, so the reader shouldn't be put off by the links. After all, it's still your post, and they don't have to click on the links!

Another tip to grow your affiliate marketing business is to be honest and only promote products you know. You want to build trust with your readers and so you must be honest with them. Link products you already use, or products that you are at least very familiar with. It doesn't exactly look good on your part if you are promoting car parts but you have no idea what parts are even in a car. It's okay if you weren't a huge fan of the product either. Go ahead and tell your readers that the product isn't your favorite, but lots of others like it. They will see you as more "real" because you aren't just selling out. No one likes a sellout.

You should have a pretty good idea of who your readers are and what they like by now. So out of all those products you like, think about which ones your readers will like too. Which products will they buy? You may love the newest Stephen King book and could totally promote the Amazon link, but if your readers are all fans of Nora Roberts, your readers won't have much interest in buying the Stephen King book.

Do not leave out brick and mortar businesses either. If there are companies that sell products that you love, don't be afraid to contact them and ask if there is a promotion you can run on your site. They may have some discount code customers can use when they shop in store or online. It's okay to think outside the box (or outside the internet in this case) and come up with unique ways to partner with companies.

Think about creating your own page for products as well. The page can have a title along the lines of "my favorite products" and can feature some of your favorite products that you have reviewed. Plug some affiliate links into the page so that readers have a place that is always right there when they want to check out a product you recommend. This is especially useful if you know readers really liked specific products you promoted. Make sure those are readily available to your followers.

Affiliate Marketing can be fun to use and it helps bring in good money. But just like advertising, you must be careful in how much you take advantage of it. Readers don't like it when bloggers focus too much on the affiliate links. They want good, content-driven posts full of actual information, not just product links for you to make money on.

Chapter 9: Selling Products

If the type of blog allows for it, you can sell products on your site. Sometimes this doesn't always work, or it takes a lot of creativity to be able to come up with ways to sell actual products. There are different types of product you can sell, however, and we will discuss how to do this.

Selling Physical Products: Crafters, this is especially useful for you! If you make your own products, you can most definitely sell them on your blog. WooCommerce is a great add-on for your blog. You can find it by going to your dashboard and looking at the add-on section. There you will find different plugins, including the ones you can use to sell products on your site. WooCommerce is the plugin that most bloggers recommend. It will walk you through creating an online store within your blog and help you to set up the products you want to sell.

Even if you don't make your own products, you can use other sites to sell products. Sites like <u>Threadless</u> let you design images that they will put on products for you. They also take care of the shipping. All you have to do it provide the link to your shop that you set up with them.

Let's say you can't make things and you just weren't gifted with artistry, there is always the option of selling third-party products. You can link products just like with affiliate marketing, or you can start your own Shopify store and link it to your blog. Shopify makes it easy to start your own online store from scratch and allows you to sell third-party products. People purchase the product from you (usually with the price increased a bit), then you buy it from a warehouse of your choosing. When you use Shopify, AliExpress is the default warehouse. The warehouse ships the products to your customers and you get to keep the profit.

Each of the methods for selling physical products can work to your advantage, but remember to stick with your niche. Sell products tailored to your readers. If you are a crafter, and your blog is about crafting, you will do fine selling handmade products. If you decide to start selling third-party motorcycle toys, your readers will probably be less than thrilled.

Digital Products: Right now, there are a lot of bloggers that sell services instead of physical products. Everywhere you look, there is a blogger promoting their "how-to" services. This book is a fitting example of that. It's a "how-to" eBook on making money blogging. There are a lot of us out there doing this: selling services to make a profit. It's a popular thing right now and there is no reason you can't get in on it!

If you blog about blogging, this is your time to shine. Everyone wants to blog! You, dear reader, are proof of this. What tips and tricks do you have to offer? Write an eBook about how to start a blog. If you know more than me, write another book on "how to make money blogging". Everyone has their own tips and tricks and can easily sell their own eBooks.

You can also sell photographs and illustrations. Do you blog about photography and know how to edit photos really well? Perfect, you can sell photos that others can use on their sites or come up with an eBook on Photoshop.

If you are not afraid of putting your face out there, start a web series about your particular niche. Sell spots for the series and be sure to offer content about your niche that people will want to hear about. Offer up seats for a big webinar you plan on hosting. Tell people there are limited seats and they need to act fast if they want to get secret tips and tricks that they won't find anywhere else.

Offer up some e-courses for free to promote your other digital products. You can use free webinars to promote your next big eBook on cute kittens. Plenty of bloggers offer free products or services in order to entice people to buy the next bigger products. They do this because it works. Give people a taste of what you have to offer, then let them know they can buy your eBook or lessons in whatever your niche may be.

Crafters will have an easier time selling digital products as well. Knitters and crocheters can easily digital patterns for unique products they make. Other crafters can sell the "how-to" for creating unique projects. Offer up a free guide to popsicle stick crafts when people buy your extensive eBook on "Crafting Christmas" (go ahead, you can heave that idea).

This will be easier to do with some niches compared to others. Remember when we talked about the horror niche being fairly untapped? It is hard to sell a lot of digital products. Not too many people want to buy an eBook on "best horror villains" or "how to become a horror fan". You are going to have to make sure you have digital products to offer that people can't easily get anywhere else. Market yourself as having information and products people won't find as easily. Make sure you have products people actually want.

Selling Services: I consider services a type of product, it just isn't tangible. Selling services can be incredibly lucrative. After all, you are not only selling a product, but also your time and energy. A lot of bloggers will sell their services. Abagail and Emylee of Think Creative Collective have grown their blogging business into a big money-making empire. They did it by selling courses on how to make money blogging and everything else involved with the blogging world. Then there are bloggers who have started to tap into a different sort of market. Instead of selling large courses in big groups, bloggers like Courtney Helena have chosen to start up one on one coaching. These bloggers offer up certain amounts of their time to individually coach other bloggers.

Offering this type of service can be very beneficial as it helps build strong relationships between you and other new bloggers. Time is valuable and you will be able to charge a pretty decent amount of money for your services. Look around and see what others charge for their blog coaching services. People love the one on one treatment and you can build a great clientele that will be willing to pay you for quality coaching.

Some bloggers also offer their services as a freelance writer. Freelance writers can write anything from blog posts to legal information. If you used to be a lawyer and now want to blog, start up a blog about legal issues and offer your services on legal matters. Plenty of bloggers are willing to pay someone to write to an air tights policy for their own blog. If you are a ghostwriter, you can sell your ghostwriting services right on your blog as well. If you have a service to sell and market yourself right, people will pay for those services.

Not sure what services you can offer? There are all kinds out there from web developer to cook. If you can type fast, sell your transcription services. If you know coding, sell your coding services. You can offer to tutor people in things or give speeches on the topics you know so well. The possibilities are endless and people will gladly pay a professional for their services.

Premium Content and Memberships: Premium content and memberships are a growing source of income for many bloggers. Do you have insider information that you can offer your subscribers? You are going to have to dig deep for this one because there is so much free information out there on the web. You will really have to know tips and tricks that aren't easily found on the internet. But if you truly have a lot of experience in an area, then you can offer premium content.

People also love memberships. They join clubs and get membership cards for everything now. There is a reason every grocery store has a membership program with perks. People love to be a part of something that offers some rewards. When you offer them a membership with rewards, people jump on it. Some bloggers offer lifetime memberships to premium content when they pay for a certain service. And it works!

Tell potential subscribers that they can get access to your insider's group on Facebook for subscribing to your blog. This makes people feel like they are special because they get to be involved in the cool kids' group. Appeal to readers' drive for belonging. Make sure the group offers insider information that won't be available on your site. Or maybe the exclusive group is just for subscribers to your blog, and it creates a place where all of your followers can chat and get to know each other. There they can talk about whatever niche happens to drive you blog and group.

The premium content needs to be worth it for the reader. No one is going to pay for mediocre content. Your premium content needs to be spectacular. That Facebook group should probably have insider content that readers won't get anywhere else. Your eBook needs to be filled with useful information. Instead of a Facebook group, try creating a chat room for your premium users. Make sure you have a bunch of offers as well so that you have something for everyone. Don't rely on one premium content offer, you will just be restricting yourself and readers. Do you have templates you can offer that are proven to increase sales? If you are a writer, maybe you have an eBook about writing you can sell to your readers, then offer a membership into a writer's only group. Offer a freebie with your premium content. You will need to give readers a really enticing offer if you want them to pay for premium content.

Chapter 10: Vlogging and Podcasts

Bloggers are no longer limited to just writing these days. Many bloggers not only keep up a blog but also get onto YouTube or start podcasts. Adding either of these options to your blogging can get you followers and money.

Vlogging: Vlogging is video blogging. People everywhere love vlogging and it can be easy once you get the hang of it. Vlogging can bring you closer to your audience and let you connect with them on a whole new level. And with how many people watch YouTube videos, there is no reason not to give it a shot.

Some of the work is already done for you now that you have your blog. You already have your name and a niche. Now, you just need to set up an account. If you are already on Google Plus, this is perfect. Google owns YouTube. You can link your accounts if you want to and get more of a following. If you don't already have an account, set one up with YouTube. It is fast and easy.

Before you start uploading videos (which, again, is super easy to do), you are going to want to get a feel for vlogging. If you have never made your own YouTube video or you don't have much experience in front of a camera, you are going to want to practice. Use your phone, your computer, a camera, etc. Start creating videos where you talk about something in your niche. Make it something you love, it will be easier to talk about it.

Experiment with moving around, moving the camera angle, where you will be looking, and sound. Remember that people are going to see your face all the time now, and they want quality video. If your phone isn't taking very good videos, time to invest in a camera. Even the cheaper ones can make awesome videos.

You should already have a brand and logo, and you are going to want to make sure your YouTube page has all of this on it. What do you want people to see when they first open your YouTube channel? You want your channel to look good, profession, and fun. People want something that looks interesting, and if there is a moment of hesitation from them, they are going to go elsewhere.

Find video editing software for your videos. Vloggers always edit videos to look better, and you will want to as well. If you are showing people how to do something, there is a good chance you are going to want to cut video out so that your viewers don't have to sit through all the boring parts. There is free editing software you can use to experiment with. Learn how to edit so that you can make your videos stand out. Just don't add too many distractions like crazy fades between scenes. You want a clean video that is also fun and easily watchable.

Research again here. Take a look at popular videos and see how they look. How long are the videos and how do the speakers present the information? Where are they filming the videos? In their house? In a studio? Pay attention to how the videos look and how they are edited. This will give you a good idea of how your videos should be presented.

Stay in touch with your subscribers by commenting back when they leave you a comment. Show your viewers that you really do care and pay attention to what they are saying. Have shout-outs to fans within your videos, let them know they have been heard. You have been working on building relationships with your readers, but your video viewers need to connect with you too.

When you show your fans your appreciation, it will prompt them to contribute more. You will start seeing more activity from viewers and they will leave more comments and like your videos. The more your viewers like you and your vlog, the more likely it is that they will also share it!

Making Money Vlogging: Google AdSense will help you here again. The concept is the same as advertising with your blog. There will be an ad on your channel and each time someone clicks it, you get paid. Now, you will only get a few cents, but it adds up when you get a lot of traffic to your channel.

Do not click on ads yourself. Google is pretty smart and will pick up on this. You will get banned from AdSense and you don't want that. Don't ask people to click on the links either. It's wrong and you don't want to point viewers in the wrong direction or make them not want to trust you.

Getting a sponsor can be extremely lucrative if you are steadily racking up the views. Sponsors pay you a certain amount to promote their product on your channel. You can come up with a flat fee and charge them a certain amount to promote that product. Check out this article by Vlog Nation to get an idea of what you should be charging from your sponsors.

You may also want to create a media kit for your YouTube channel as well. Put in it all the same things you did for your blogging media kit, only this time, plug in stats from your channel. You want a nice document describing how well your channel is doing. This will help you get sponsors so that you can make the big bucks. Include some stats for your blog too. Make sure that you are able to show that your linked blog is also doing well. In your YouTube media kit, you will want to include (if applicable) how well you have done on past sponsorships and any testimonials from anyone who has worked with you in the past.

Selling an eBook through your channel is how a lot of vloggers make money too. We discussed this a bit in previous chapters as well. You don't have to only sell products through your blog. If you set up a YouTube channel, then promote your items for sale on that platform as well. Why not have it on both sites? And if you decide to start writing about how to get a YouTube channel going, you can sell that eBook right there on your channel!

You can also look into selling your merchandise. Selling merch can be huge for your blog and vlog. Come up with a high-quality brand or logo, and you can get it put on anything! There are stores out there like <u>Teespring</u> and <u>Spreadshirt</u> that will help you design clothing, t-shirts, accessories, etc. You can advertise these on your site (minimally at first) and direct viewers to your collection. There they can buy merch with your logo on it. You get a commission from the sale and you don't have to take care of any of the shipping!

Merchandise Tip: Come up with a logo or brand that is appealing to your viewers. Make it something they would be proud to wear. You want your viewers to look at your t-shirt line and think "oh wow, that's cool!". It needs to be something people see and want to buy. You can research what other vloggers are selling, or you can simply ask your viewers to help come up designs with you. Offer a contest to see who comes up with the best designs and reward the winner with something (free merch?). And be patient. People are not going to start buying up products right off the bat. Let them get to know you and get a feel for your brand. They will buy, you just need to give them time.

Podcasts: Podcasts are getting increasingly popular. How many times do you hear from your friends that you need to start listening to someone's podcast? They have grown into a huge money-making, information sharing monster. A podcast is an audio file that you can listen to by downloading it or streaming it through a website or app. It is typically presented in a series and you can listen to it as you would watch a television series.

Podcasts are great because you can choose what content you want to listen to. There are sports podcasts, spooky podcasts, how-to podcast, and much much more. A podcast can be great for those of you that don't want to do video and show their faces to the world. It's okay, some of us have stage fright. With podcast on the rise, now is a wonderful time to start thinking of getting one going to work with your blog. If you want to really get into all the information about what a podcast is and can be, check out this article.

Again, you should already have a niche and logo ready, so half the work is done. Next, you will want to make sure you have something you will be able to speak into that sounds good! You will then record audio clips onto your computer and save each file with a good descriptive name. You will then upload your file to a server through the web. This lets apps and websites locate your files and allows users to listen to your podcasts. Pat Flynn has a great tutorial page you can check out here. He goes into detail on how to get your podcast going with some informative videos.

Making Money with Podcasts: Not everyone has a podcast to make money, but many people who start one, or have been doing one, want some extra income. Just as with vlogging and blogging, you can get sponsors for your podcasts. You can do this the same way as you do with blogging and a YouTube channel. Find companies you know and trust, or products you know and trust, to review. Ask for a certain amount, a flat fee, or a commission and get paid by sponsors for your content.

You can work with affiliates and make a commission off of products. Amazon has a great affiliate program, or you can start selling the third-party as we discussed previously. There is an option to sell content, premium content, eBooks, and merch. Again, making money through a podcast is similar to YouTube and blogging. You will just need to figure out which method works best for you and run with it.

With a podcast, you offer premium episodes of your show or exclusive access to a community page. If you really develop a strong relationship with your listeners, you can ask for donations. This is if you truly have passionate and devoted fans. Super fans are willing to donate to help keep their show running. If enough people donate, you can make enough to at least cover the costs of running your podcast. Offer paid courses on learning to podcast, or on whatever your niche is. Maybe you know a lot about reviewing products. You can charge a small fee for courses or an eBook on how to be a world-class reviewer.

If you were to combine your blog with a podcast, or with a YouTube channel, think about how this would affect your profits. You have the potential to earn from two (or three if you are really ambitious) streams, which could possibly mean double the income. You will reach even more people when you don't stick to just writing a blog. Expand your blog, and you reach entirely new groups of people. Not everyone likes to read, and not everyone wants to watch a video. There is no reason not to give podcasts and YouTube a shot.

Podcasting can cost some money to start, so be prepared to invest some. You may want a microphone for your computer so that you have better sound. Maybe you want better software for your podcast. You may need to invest a little to get going, but as long as you work hard, you will make up for the amount you send and then some. You may end up spending a little for you podcast each month, so keep that in mind when you think about making money. You at least need to be able to make up for what you lose in expenses.

Chapter 11: SEO

SEO stands for Search Engine Optimization, and it is crucial to getting your blog recognized. When you write up your blog posts and add images, search engines use the information and keywords to rank your posts and pages in their listings. If you do a search for "best baby names in 2017", you get a top result from babycenter.com. How did they get to be number one? Disregard the ad, we can talk about that later. Have you thought about how sites get to be the top search result? They don't buy their way there, or else it would be featured in the ads and not the actual results. And no, it's not some kind of wizardry.

Getting into the top search results is a lot of work and you really must hone your SEO skills. The top results are there because they contain just the right keywords and content. Not only do they contain that perfect keyword, they are also popular and get a lot of traffic. SEO makes sure that your site is recognized by search engines and so that you can get more organize traffic to your site.

We will go over some of the basics to get you on your way, but know that there is a lot of information out there on SEO and how to perfect it. This is something that is always changing as the internet as well as search engines change and get smarter. Moz.com has a great guide to SEO and their site offers guides and information on virtually everything that has to do with blogging.

Search Engines: Search engines are pretty damn smart. They are able to sift through links and follow them along, searching for valuable content and storing it for later use. This way they can go back to it to get you answers when you do a search. They gather the most relevant information first and then sort it by popularity. Meaning, if your site may be relevant to a search, but without popularity, you probably won't get ranked where a user can see.

One of the first things you can do is see what search engines see with your site. This will help you to see if the search engine is catching any of the valuable content you want it to. Remember that the search engines are only capable of so much! Take a look at the cached version of your site. It may look similar to what you normally see, or it may look completely different. What you are seeing is what the search engine sees. If you don't see any of your rich information on the cashed site, you have some work to do. If the search engine isn't picking up any of your essential information, rethink your wording and adjust it to more normal wording.

Be sure to link your work as well. If you are not creating links within your site search engines will stop where the links stop. They rely on those links to navigate your site. Don't leave the search engines hanging, and be sure to add links to your other pages throughout the site.

Keywords are going to be your friends from now on. Start practicing using them and get familiar with how to use them. A keyword is a word or phrase that is the focus of your post. It should describe what the post is about and should be in the beginning of the title.

Your keyword is what search engines will use to see if your posts or site is relevant to what is being searched on the internet. Therefore, make your keywords something someone is searching for! Don't make your keyword "dogs".

That is so generic, there are literally thousands of sites that will always get ranked higher than yours. Instead, narrow it down. What is your post about? Is it about types of dogs? Is it about why mixed breeds are the best kinds of dogs? Your keyword should be something along the lines of "Mixed breeds are the best dogs", or "why are mixed breed dogs better", or change the wording to something like "why are mutts good dogs".

The idea here is to come up with keywords that not only describe what your post is about but are also what people are actually searching for. You'll have to do some searching yourself and see what people are looking for in terms of what you are writing about. Come up with keywords that will get you noticed by search engines, but are what actual people would search. Want to see if your keyword is searchable? Do a search of it yourself!

This includes the ALT text for images. This is the text that search engines use in order to read the picture if they aren't able to process the image. You will find the ALT text when editing the images you are inserting into your blog, or when you add general media files to your account. There will be a section that says ALT text, and here you should use your keyword to describe the image. Make sure the description is to the point. Search engines will use this to find your images as well.

When you come up with the URL to your post (you can edit this when you edit the SEO section of your post), keep the keywords toward the front of the URL and title of the post. Most search engines will limit the title to sixty-five to seventy-five characters. After that, they cut you off. So, try to keep the titles short and descriptive.

You should also use the keyword a few times throughout the post, with one placement of a keyword within the first few sentences. Make sure it flows nicely too. You don't want your post to look like you forced those words into your post.

Still need some help in determining if the keywords you are using are, right? There are tools out there that can help you with that. Take a look at Moz's Keyword Explorer. Here, you can search keywords and learn how well that keyword will do. Moz offers tips and ways to use that keyword. Go, take a look at it and do a search yourself. It will let you know how difficult it will be for you to rank higher than competitors and how often your keyword is searched.

With search engines changing and updating all the time, one thing you can count on is that having a good, user friendly-site will always help your rankings. Search engines are even able to judge if a site has quality content or not! Make sure that your site brings out positive emotion in users and creates a fun, thoughtful environment for them.

Tools for Getting Search Engines to Notice You: There are tools out there that can help search engines find your site easier as well. We won't be going too deep into these because the information on them is extensive and requires much more than a section of a book. But you are more than welcome to look into these tools.

A sitemap is a list of information that you set up to help search engines crawl your site easier. XML-sitemaps.com has all kinds of information and can help you set up a sitemap for your blog. Using sitemaps like this makes it possible for search engines to find content on your site that they may not have been to fins on their own.

You can also utilize robots.txt, meta robots, rel="Nofollow", and rel="canonical". These tools are a little more complicated and are used by more experienced bloggers. Feel free to look into these after you have your blog up and running and be able to learn more about your blog. You can get more information on these tools through the Moz website here.

You can also enter information into the consoles of search engines and see how your site is performing. Moz has a really great tool called Open Site Explorer that will show you a lot of information on your site, including links and how well your site is ranking. You can get a lot of free information from this tool, but you will have to pay for a membership if you really want to utilize all it has to offer.

Google has a free option to use that can tell you if they have found errors while crawling your site. Take a minute to look at their search console. You will see that once you plug in your website, Google starts to analyze your site and gives you ways of improving your site's searchability. If that all seems confusing, take advantage of their guides and tutorials. Google is great at guiding you through how to use their tools.

Be sure to track the progress you make and how your site is performing. You can use Moz or Google, or whatever analytics software you choose. It is good to pay attention to the traffic coming into your blog, but also how search engines are finding your site. If you are not getting enough organic traffic (non-paid traffic), then you will know that you need to adjust your SEO strategies. Remember to focus on keywords that other people would use when searching for your content.

SEO Made Easy: The platform you are using should already have SEO tools built in. Look through the available add-ons and you find SEO tools to help you as you write. One of the most popular plugins is <u>Yoast</u>. Yoast is a plugin that works while you type your posts. It lets you know in real time if your post or page is search engine optimized. You will see a little traffic light on the bottom of the post you are working on, and two check boxes to the right. The checkboxes will show you whether your readability is good and if your SEO is good. You want both boxes to be checked with a green Y if you want your SEO to be good.

At the bottom of the post you are working on, you will also see an SEO section. Here, you are able to modify the URL, your keywords, and the description of your post. You will see the little traffic light change colors depending on whether your post is search engine optimized or not.

You can also use the All in One SEO Pack plugin for your blog. It does a lot of the same things Yoast does but without the pretty colors. Both plugins offer a free version you can use first. If you like one enough, you can buy the premium version and get a few more features that can better your SEO.

SEO can get tricky and there is a lot involved. You don't have to get crazy with it to be a successful blogger. As a matter of fact, don't spend too much time trying to optimize each post for search engines to find you. All you will do is create a post that looks weird and appears write for the search engine instead of the reader. It is important to know how to utilize SEO, but remember it isn't everything.

SEO Tips: Google is starting to move away from focusing in on just keywords. While it is important to utilize keywords well, don't put all your energy in writing for keywords. Get really good at the subject you are writing about and then modify your keywords. Your content is more important than trying to come up with good keywords. Google (and other search engines) are getting smarter and are learning to recognize useful content, spamming, and long-tailed keywords.

Make sure that you are backlinking to reputable sites. When citing your information and instructing your readers to look at other content, you want to send them sites that will give them good information as well. Your readers need to know that they can trust you and your judgment.

You also want your content to be worthy of backlinking. You want your content to be worthy of sharing. Creating great content and quotes can get your site noticed by more people. You can potentially get others to link your blog in something they are writing. This will boost your SEO and get you noticed more by the search engines. The more quality backlinks you have, the better your chances of being ranked higher by search engines. Remember, organic growth is best because it increases your SEO and rankings!

Chapter 12: Common Mistakes in Blogging

New and pro bloggers alike are not immune from mistakes when blogging. So many bloggers find themselves making mistakes here and there. The key is recognizing when you've made those mistakes and correcting them. With how often the internet and people's interests change, you can find yourself slipping up at any point in your blogging career. Here are some common mistakes bloggers make and what you can do to avoid them.

Do Not Clutter Your Site: Have you ever been to a website where there was stuff everywhere? Like a dirty kid's room, they have ads and banners and videos and pictures scattered all over the home page. Music starts playing from some ad and you can't figure out which ad it's coming from. You know there are blog posts in there somewhere, but you are afraid to click on one because it may just be another ad. Or it may lead you to another page that is just as unappealing as the home page.

This happens all the time to newer bloggers. They want to sell ad space, but also want to fill their sidebars, headers, and footers with as much information or advertisements as possible. I get it too, you want to make money right away and you have been told by other bloggers to put this here and that there. But remember, clutter is unattractive and will only drive away readers. No one wants to see a ton of ads or even too many links or side notes on your page. Keep it simple and clean. If you must have ads, only use some that are related to your blog so that they aren't so distracting.

The focus of your blog should be the blog! Ads are background noise both literally and figuratively. Too much background noise is distracting and takes away from the enjoyable content of your site. On that note, don't use ads that automatically play music or commercials when readers view your site. Have you ever visited a site that had a video automatically start playing? Not only is it annoying because you are being forced to listen and watch something instead of reading what you went to the site to read in the first place, but the entire site slows to a crawl. Those video ads that automatically play slow down websites so much. You will lose readers before they even get a chance to view any of your content. Don't use those ads.

Color Schemes and Fonts: When customizing your blog, it can be tempting to change the screen color to black with a bright yellow font. Yes, we all remember the Myspace days when that was fun to do. But society is on computers all the time now and the screens are hard enough on our eyes. Don't make it worse by using dark screens with a bright font. Darker screens cause more eye strain, and the bright fonts are awful to read. All About Vision recommends that you should be reading screens that are the same brightness of the room you are in, and using screens with a white background and black font. The same article also recommends looking away from your computer every twenty minutes, so make sure your pages are also to the point.

Even if you are using a white background, do not use bright lettering! Stick to darker fonts as they are easier to read. Look at amateur sites where the screen is bright white, and the font is bright green. It hurts to look at. People need darker colors to make focusing easier. If your font is too bright, no one will want to read your post.

Fonts need to be legible. I shouldn't have to explain this one, but make sure your words are easy to read. There are so many fonts out there that are fun to use and still look good. So as discussed previously, please use legible fonts and not ones that people will struggle to follow.

Do Not Plagiarize: This sounds so simple until you realize how easy it is to plagiarize without even knowing you're doing it! Plagiarizing consists of writing content that is too close to some else's or is exactly what someone else wrote. It also consists of using images that are not your own. Now, here is why so many bloggers are guilty of plagiarism and don't even realize it.

Bloggers tend to plagiarize images the most. They do a search for certain images and choose one that works for their post. Then they download it and plug the image into their blog post. They credit the source and leave it at that. It sounds good, and after all, we do it on Pinterest all the time, right? Well, this is still considered plagiarism. You cannot use someone else's image without permission! Even if you cite the source within your post, you are plagiarizing as long as you do not have written consent from the original owner to use the image.

If you find images you really want to use, you are going to have to start getting permission. You can most definitely reach out to people and ask for permission, but this can be time-consuming. Many successful bloggers use stock images to remedy this problem.

Stock images are images that have been sold to companies to use without the original owner's permission. They give their rights to pictures up so that others can use the images. There are a number of sites that have stock images you can use for your site. Free sites such as Pexels.com offer tons of images that you can get for free. This can work well if you are on a fixed budget for now.

Bigger sites like Shutterstock and Getty Images have even more images you can use, but you will have to pay for the images. And you will still need to credit the site with your photo. The benefit of paying for images is that you can get a lot of quality images without having to worry about plagiarism. The downside is that these images are not cheap. You may wind up paying a lot of money to these sites for their images. Of course, when you are making a lot of money with your blog, you won't mind dishing out some for images.

Another way to avoid plagiarizing images it to create your own. Hire a photographer or learn how to take good photos. Photographylife.com has great tips on how to better your photography skills. Learning how to take great photos will save you from having to search for images on those stock images sites. Take pictures of everything. If you have a camera, bring it everywhere. If not, your phone will most likely have a camera and I am sure you rarely put your camera down. Take photos often and learn how to edit them.

There are tons of apps now that will help you to edit photos. Some are free and others you have to pay for. Remember, though, that you get what you pay for. Many bloggers love PicMonkey. They have a free option and a paid subscription. Naturally, you can do much more with the paid version. PicMonkey can be easier to use if you are new to editing and offers many tools in order to create your perfect images. Photoshop is another great photo editing service that many bloggers use. Get to know it and you will start to create great images that you don't need permission to use!

For your words, you are going to want to check to make sure they haven't already been said by someone else. There are a number of sites on the internet that will check your work for you. Sites such as smallseotools.com and paperrater.com offer free plagiarism checks for your content. All you have to do is copy and paste.

Plagiarism is never okay, even if you didn't know you were doing it. If you think that you have accidentally plagiarized someone else's images or work, please do yourself a favor and fix it. Even if you think no one will notice, just get it fixed. Somewhere down the line when you are way more popular, someone may notice that you used an image without permission, and you don't want all that legal hassle.

Don't Use Big Words: Look, we all know you're smart. You started a blog and know a lot about your niche. But you don't need to use huge words or try to make yourself smarter. Using too much technical writing will either confuse readers or bore them. We aren't in high school anymore and no one wants to read a term paper again! Write as if you are talking to a friend in a language you would use in a normal conversation. Keeping it light and easy will keep your readers engaged.

Back Up Your Information with Sources: You may have a lot to say on a subject, and that's great! But how do your readers know that you know what you are talking about? Blathering on and on about something will hold no merit if you can't back up what you are saying. So, you think calicos are the best cats and write you wrote an entire post about why they are the best. Readers may like the post, but they are going to want to know why you think calicos are the best. What are your reasons for this opinion? What evidence do you have that backs up your claim?

Readers want to know where your information comes from. Be sure to cite sources throughout your post where it needs it. Get to know hyperlinks and use them throughout the post. This gives readers a link to the information you used so they can look into it themselves.

Don't Focus on Perfecting Your Blog: So many bloggers make the mistake of aiming for perfection. They overanalyze every aspect of their blog from images to posts to editing. Your work doesn't have to be perfect! Quit spending so much time tweaking and making sure everything is just right. You are human, your readers are human, and they want to see how human you are. Let there be little mistakes, let there be little goofs. It's humorous and shows the genuine, personal side of you. Don't worry about getting every joke right, and getting the wording just right. You will drive yourself crazy perfecting your posts. At some point, you need to settle for what you have and post it.

Chapter 13: Tips and Tricks

Every blogger learns tips and tricks along the way. Many bloggers have to learn some of these on their own and struggle during their journey. Good news for, I'm going to put these tips and tricks into this one book for you.

Write for Your Readers: Here's your first tip. Instead of trying so hard to write for SEO, write for your readers first. When you start focusing too much on SEO, you forget to write for your readers. Write your post for them, giving them the content they are looking for. If you're writing about blogging, help your readers by giving them the blogging tips they need. Then go back and edit for SEO, but don't make that your focus. When you start focusing on SEO first, your posts start to come out too structured and they tend to not flow very well.

Write for Yourself: Why did you start your blog in the first place? Hopefully, it was a passion first, then you realized you could make good money. You have to have a passion for something before you can make money from it. And you will need to write for yourself first if you want people to follow. This ties in with not writing for SEO. Write a post that you really wanted to write. Your passion for the subject will shine throw and others will notice.

When you write for yourself first, you will also post more often and have quality content. When you actually want to write about things, you will get excited to write. You'll do the research, you'll put in the time, and you'll post regularly. You'll get more readers and keep readers with this kind of blogging strategy.

Don't ignore SEO either, please. You can blog for yourself and readers first, but if you want your posts to get ranked with search engines, you will still want to work on some SEO. Making it second will keep you interested in blogging. Nothing is worse than losing interest in a passion because it became too much work.

Local SEO: If your blog is also a business, this one will help you get noticed a lot. But use common sense here. If you are strictly blogging from your house and don't want to see things, be careful what information you are putting out there on the web for all to see.

Google lists local places first in a search. When you search for a business on Google, notice that all the local places that have to do with your search come up first. For example, if you were to do a search for Best Buy, you will get an ad, but your nearest Best Buy stores show up first in the search results, then the actual website. This works for all Google searches.

If you have a business and want it to show up locally for people, add your address to your website and your social media accounts. Google will use that and start listing your business near the top (if you are still using proper SEO strategies). If you want to really boost your ranking potential, get yourself listed on sites that rate companies, such as Angie's List. The more people that give you good stars or complimentary reviews, the higher your local business will rank.

Do Your Research: How many times have we gone over this throughout the book? Doing your research is the key to having a successful blog. You must make sure that there is a market for what you are trying to bring to the table. If the market is already saturated, time to rethink what it is you are trying to do with your blog. Don't be afraid of digging deeper and coming up with a more narrowed version of your original niche idea.

Research your competitors. See what they are doing with their blogs and check out their ranking. What are they selling? Why is their blog so successful? Don't be afraid to use some of the strategies they are using either.

Do a Google search (or Bing or Yahoo) using some keywords for your niche. Take a look at the top websites that pop up. Go ahead and go to those sites and take a look around. What are they doing that is making their blogs so successful? What are they selling? What are the page setups? See what their average word count is. Look around and see what it is they are doing. Check out links, contributors, how often they post. This can all help you get an idea of what you need to do with your blog to get ranked like they do.

Please remember, do not steal the content! It's okay to check out the competition, but you cannot use their materials and steal their work. It's not only wrong, but search engines find out and you end up punished. You don't want your site tagged by search engines for taking content. It is very hard to come back from.

Brand Yourself: This can be a be a huge contributor in earning an income. Your brand is what will sell people on you. Your brand is what people will know you for. You will need to make sure that your content is great and you stick with your niche. You need to be an authority on your subject matter.

Create an image that you can use for a logo, or just for selling merchandise. You will want something that stands out but looks good. It needs to be something that people want. When you create a brand for yourself, and you come up with some images that people can associate with you, you can gain even more followers and earn more income.

Site Speed: Do you know how fast your site speed is? Have you tested how smoothly posts open or fast users can switch to a new page? People want to see a site that moves quickly and smoothly. Lag will lose readers fast. Go online and take a look at how your site is running. Recruit friends and family to go through your blog and ask them how they feel about the speed of the site. If there is any kind of lag, glitching, or slowness, you will have to go back and fix it. This shouldn't be an issue if you are using one of the good, paid hosting sites and WordPress.

Get Comfortable with Voice Search: Voice search is growing fast and Google is adapting to it. People are using Google, Siri, and Cortana to do searches on the internet. You will need to adapt to this as well. When people do voice searches, they do it a little different than typing in what they want to know. Modify for keywords and SEO strategies to account for this change in wording now. People speak of their smart systems now like a normal person. Listen to someone talk to Siri. They treat it as if it were a person and do searches the same. Think about how you will modify your keywords to make it sounds more natural and what someone would ask their voice search software.

Don't Focus It All on Google: I think we all know how big Google is. Google is a leader when it comes to developing software and many bloggers tailor their blogs for the Google search engine. But realistically, Google is not the only search engine out there and you will have readers who don't use Google. Many people still use Bing and new search engines are being developed all the time. They may not be as big as the big boys, but they are out there. Get to know what other search engines exist and do a little research. Find out what drives their ranking system and try incorporating some of that into your blog as well.

Quit Listening to Everyone Else: I know, this goes against the entire book. So, read the book then do this. New bloggers tend to read everything they can about marketing, SEO, how to make money, etc. The problem with all of that? You're not doing! Go ahead and learn how to set up a blog, learn how to make money from it. Learn some SEO strategies. You will need them all. But don't spend all of your time trying to learn everything there is to know about blogging. You will drive yourself crazy trying to listen to all of the advice and you'll find yourself sitting there will a pile of information but no content for your blog.

Remember too that blogging is an ever-changing industry. It will morph all the time. SEO strategies change, Google changes, search engines change. By the time you are done researching all the best advice for this year, it will have changed by the next year and you'll wind up trying to do all the research again.

Plus, what worked for one successful blogger didn't work for another one. Go ahead and take a look at the top tips from pro bloggers. Their number one tips vary according to which ones helped their blogs succeed. Some insist that making your blog mobile friendly is the number one key to blog performance, while others insist email marketing is number one. You are going to have to take the time to see what strategies work best for you, and which ones don't. Keep the other strategies in the back of your mind should you decide to work on them later, but focus on what is working for you! It's your blog and only you will know what is going to make you feel successful.

Chapter 14: Some Advice for You, the Blogger

Be Prepared to Fail: That's not a very comforting tip, is it? The reason for it though is that there are many bloggers who have failed at least once before really hitting it big. There is a chance that your first blog will go nowhere and you will either wind up starting all over again or redoing your entire first blog. But remember that this is okay! It means you are learning what works and what doesn't. Learn from the mistakes you may have made and start again. Some of the most successful bloggers failed a few times before they hit success.

Be Prepared for a Wait: Blogging is a not a success overnight. It just doesn't happen that way. Anyone who tries to tell you that you can make ten thousand dollars in your first week is trying to sell you something (don't trust those people). There are many successful bloggers out there that will tell you it takes time to make money. But once it finally takes off, you will bring in a nice income. Be ready to work hard with no payoff for a little while. Some bloggers don't see a dime until they have been blogging for a year. You may hit success within a few months, and that is great! Just be mentally prepared for the wait.

Join Facebook Groups: There are several Facebook groups out there that are focused on blogging. Join them. Join a bunch to see what they are about, choose the ones that really help you the most, and stick with them. Many of these groups are run by successful bloggers who have a lot of great advice for you. Bloggers are generally tend to be nice people, so connect with them. See what they do that makes them so successful. Joining a group also connects you more personally with those successful bloggers. You can pick their brains and ask them advice.

Another wonderful thing about joining a Facebook group is you can get support from other bloggers. Blogging can get lonely, but it doesn't mean you have to be alone. Many of the groups offer a safe place for you to vent, ask questions, and get help from other bloggers. Sometimes you will need a bit of encouragement from a fellow blogger. These groups will give you the emotional and technical support you need to be a success.

Invest in a Planner or Journal: A simple daily planner will do, or you can go online and search for productivity planners. The productivity planners are great for beginners because you can set goals and keep track of everything involved with your life and blog. <u>Conquer Your Year</u> is a great planner that will help you break down your days, weeks, and months into achievable goals and it will help you reach them.

If you don't want to invest in a productivity planner, a weekly planner will do the trick. Set goals for yourself including when you will publish posts. You will want to keep track of how you are doing and post on a schedule if you can. Keep track of how you feel too. Writing everything down can help tremendously with keeping you on track.

You can use the planners or even an app to keep track of your daily schedule as well. It is incredibly easy to get distracted these days. Social media is on your face, your phone is constantly making noises, and life gets distracting. Set up time blocks for your day to keep yourself occupied and distraction free. For example, you can set up time frames devoted to blogging, but then give yourself a block of time to play around on Facebook. Then devote a block of time to promoting on social media, then give yourself time for exercise or a cup of coffee. Giving yourself smaller, manageable tasks will help keep you focused and determined.

Reward Yourself: Look, blogging is a lot of work, and in the beginning, there isn't much payout. You need a reason to keep your head up and a payout of your own. Reward yourself when you reach a major milestone. Maybe, in the beginning, you can treat yourself a manicure after you completed two blog posts. Maybe after a while, you get yourself a nice dinner after your first one hundred subscribers. Give yourself better rewards for accomplishing bigger goals. This will keep your morale up and it will feel even better when you've crushed your goals.

Lastly, Have Fun: Blogging should be fun, not a chore. When it becomes a chore, it shows in your posts. You started blogging because you enjoy it. Keep it enjoyable. Write for you, and it will show through your words. Don't get yourself wrapped up in all the technical stuff (unless you want to of course!). Have fun with your blog, make it your own, and remember why you started in the first place; because it is fun!

Conclusion

Thanks for reading this book. It was full of a lot of information and hopefully, you found it useful. This book was designed to make it easy for you to navigate the sections so that you can refer back to them as needed.

Blogging can be time-consuming, but it is worth it! Hopefully, you found everything you need to get started in your blogging adventure. While there is a lot more information on the internet, this book was meant to give you everything you need to get started and on your way to making good money!

Keep at it and don't give up. Have fun with your blog and remember to put that fun first. Your next steps are to keep blogging and stay up to date with the latest trends in blogging. Have fun!

Finally, if you found this book useful in any way, a review on Amazon is always appreciated!

Made in the USA
Lexington, KY
16 July 2018